12
Fabulously Funny
Folktale Plays

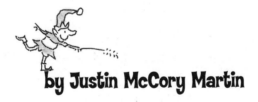

by Justin McCory Martin

NEW YORK • TORONTO • LONDON • AUCKLAND • SYDNEY
MEXICO CITY • NEW DELHI • HONG KONG • BUENOS AIRES

Teaching *Resources*

To Brett, Colleen, and Cy—
good folk who enjoy a well-told tale

Cover design by Jason Robinson
Interior design by Melinda Belter
Cover and interior artwork by Mike Gordon

ISBN: 0-439-51762-1
Copyright © 2004 by Justin McCory Martin
All rights reserved. Published by Scholastic Inc.
Printed in the U.S.A.

5 6 7 8 9 10   40   11 10 09 08 07 06

Contents

Introduction 4

Stone Slop 5
(based on "Stone Soup")

Aladdin and the Magic Pickle Jar 10
(based on "Aladdin and the Magic Lamp")

The June Bug and the Flea 16
(based on "The Grasshopper and the Ant")

The Prince Frog 21
(based on "The Frog Prince")

Queen Midas 25
(based on "King Midas")

Jack and the Giant Sunflower 31
(based on "Jack and the Beanstalk")

Claynocchio 36
(based on "Pinocchio")

Clinky Planky Tenbo 41
(based on "Tikki Tikki Tembo")

Three Silly Goats Gruff 46
(based on "Three Billy Goats Gruff")

The Elves and Young Stu Baker 50
(based on "The Elves and the Shoemaker")

Thaddeus Thumb 56
(based on "Tom Thumb")

The Pig Who Cried Wolf 61
(based on "The Boy Who Cried Wolf")

Introduction

Fractured folktales make reading come alive. Everyone knows stories such as *Pinocchio* and *Jack and the Beanstalk*. Twist them around, turn them on their heads, and you have something new and exciting that can stretch students' imaginations. This book features a dozen classic tales retold as wacky plays that can be read aloud in the classroom.

Fractured folktales are great for rainy days or anytime. Kids get a kick out of them, and it's a great way to build reading confidence. What's more, performing these plays will help students with fluency, comprehension, and vocabulary development. This book includes *The Prince Frog*, a new version of "The Frog Prince." In the memorable original, a frog gets a kiss and turns into a prince. This time around, a prince gets a kiss and turns into a frog. There's also such fractured fare as *Aladdin and the Magic Pickle Jar*, *Queen Midas*, and *Three Silly Goats Gruff*.

The plays are also meant to help unleash creativity. For example, seeing the familiar "Boy Who Cried Wolf" transformed into the fractured *Pig Who Cried Wolf* can help students see the value of twists and surprises.

Fostering a playful imagination is one of the surest routes to creativity. In fact, some of the greatest flights of fancy are simply fractured forms of earlier versions. What is *Star Wars* if not a fractured science-fiction version of an old-time Western?

Each play is accompanied by a teacher's guide that includes a bit of history and a plot summary of the original tales, which hail from different eras and from different regions—China, the Middle East, even ancient Greece. To further involve students in the tales, there are also discussion questions and writing prompts, as well as vocabulary boosters.

Enjoy these fractured folktales!

—Justin McCory Martin

Stone Slop

based on "Stone Soup"

CHARACTERS
Narrator • Monster • Five Townspeople • Monster Friends

Narrator: Once upon a time, there was a monster. His teeth were sharp and snaggly. But he was a friendly monster. The people in the town were not afraid of him. One time he was very hungry. He looked around his cave but could find no food. There was nothing but a single round stone.

    Suddenly, the monster had an idea. Maybe, if he was very clever, he could convince the townspeople to add other ingredients besides the stone. In that way, the stone could be turned into a meal.

Monster: Knock, knock, knock.

First Townsperson: Who's there?

Monster *(in a goofy voice):* It's the monster.

First Townsperson *(opening the door):* Well, hello there, monster. It's very nice to see you.

Monster: I'm making stone slop. It is going to be delicious. I already have the most important ingredient, this stone. But if I add a few more things, it will be just right.

First Townsperson: What else do you need?

Monster: Well, it's almost ready to eat. But if I could just borrow a bowl filled with liquid, it would be perfect. Any old bowl would be fine. It can be cracked or dirty. Any liquid is fine, too: grape juice, sour milk, mouthwash.

Narrator: The townsperson went back into the house and got an old bowl and filled it with prune juice. Then the townsperson handed it to the monster, who dropped the stone into the juice with a plunk.

Monster *(taking a slurp):* Mmm, this is very, very good. Would you like a taste?

First Townsperson: Uh, I don't think so.

Monster: Well, I'll just be on my way then. Thank you very much.

Narrator: The monster walked to a second house in town and knocked until someone answered the door.

Monster: I'm making stone slop. It is going to be very, very tasty. I already have the most important ingredient, this stone, plus I have prune juice and this beautiful bowl. If I could just borrow a spoon and an item of clothing, it would be perfect. Any old spoon is fine. Any item of clothing is also fine: a T-shirt, a wool scarf, a cowboy hat.

Narrator: The townsperson went back into the house and got a spoon and a pair of mismatched socks. The monster dropped the socks into the bowl and took a big spoonful.

Monster: Oh, this is good. One brown sock and one black sock, an excellent selection. Would you like a taste?

Second Townsperson: No, please. I just ate something and I'm all full.

Monster: Suit yourself. Well, I'll just be moving along.

Narrator: The monster walked to a third house. The family was having a garage sale.

Monster: I'm making stone slop. It's almost finished. I already have the most important ingredient, this stone, plus prune juice and two yummy mismatched socks. If you could just spare an item from your garage sale, it would be perfect. Anything is fine. That old baseball trading card looks scrumptious!

Third Townsperson: Well, I'm hoping to sell this trading card for a quarter. But I think I have something I can give you for your stone slop.

Narrator: The villager handed the monster an old wind-up alarm clock.

Monster: Very nice. A clock adds something crunchy to my meal. Can I offer you a bite?

Third Townsperson: Uh, no, thanks. I really have to get back to work at this garage sale.

Monster: Good luck. I'll just mosey along.

Narrator: The monster continued along the street. At the next house over, he found someone in the garage working on a car.

Monster: I'm making stone slop. It is very nearly finished. I already have the most important ingredient, this stone, plus prune juice, two mismatched socks, and an alarm clock. I see you are working on your car. If you could spare an auto part, it would be great. Anything is fine: a fender, some bolts, a few drops of motor oil for seasoning.

Narrator: The townsperson handed the monster a flat tire.

Monster: How tasty! And look how it floats in the prune juice just like a big fat dumpling. Would you like to try it?

Fourth Townsperson: I'll bet it is delicious. But I don't want to spoil my appetite before dinner.

Monster: That means more for me. Well, I'll be on my merry monster way.

Narrator: The monster walked on and came to a house where someone was working in the garden.

Monster: I'm making stone slop. It is almost perfect. I already have the most important ingredient, this stone, plus prune juice, two mismatched socks, an alarm clock, and a flat tire. I see that you are working in your garden. If you could just spare something, it would be so helpful. Anything is fine: an old rake, your garden hose, some rotten vegetables.

Narrator: The townsperson bent down, dug up several shovelfuls of dirt, and dumped them into the monster's bowl.

Monster: Dirt! What a treat! There is nothing like dirt to really bring out the flavor in a fine stone slop. Would you like to give it a try?

Fifth Townsperson: No, thanks. I'm on this new diet and I'm trying to avoid eating dirt.

Monster: Yes, soil can be very rich. I'll just be monster-ing along. Get it! Monster-ing along, tee-hee-hee.

Narrator: The monster returned to his cave with a bowl, a spoon, prune juice, mismatched socks, an alarm clock, a flat tire, some dirt, and of course, a stone. It was a perfect stone slop. All the monsters from the neighboring caves were there, too, hungry for a taste.

Monster Friends *(all talking at once):* Mmmm . . . stone slop! . . . This is perfect! I have to get your recipe! . . . Hey, you have to share! Let me have a bite of the brown sock! . . . I can't believe people gave these things away! People have no taste! . . . Let me eat the stone! . . . No, me, I want to eat the stone!

The End

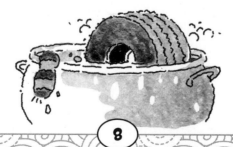

Stone Slop

History of the Tale

Stone Slop is based on "Stone Soup," a traditional European folktale. In the original, a clever and hungry stranger arrives at a farmhouse with nothing but a stone. The farmer and his wife invite the stranger inside. The stranger asks if they have ever tried stone soup. Then he starts gathering ingredients for what he promises will be a delicious dish. The couple gives him chicken broth, carrots, turnips, and spices. Finally, the stranger announces that the stone soup is ready to eat. Sure enough, it is delicious.

Vocabulary Boosters

This story contains several words that may be new to students:

ingredients (*noun, plural*): the parts or pieces of a mixture

scrumptious (*adj.*): extremely delicious

mosey (*verb, slang*): to move along in a relaxed way

Discussion Starters

● The monster and his friends thought the slop was delicious. But the slop was made out of items that people did not want, such as mismatched socks and a flat tire. An old saying goes: "One man's trash is another man's treasure." Ask students: *Do you think this is true? Are there items that other people might throw away that you would find extremely useful?*

● To make stone slop, it was necessary to gather various ingredients. Invite children to think of a dish such as a large pizza with everything on it. Have students take turns naming ingredients that should be included.

Writing Prompts

● A clever person—or monster—can create something from nothing. In *Stone Slop*, a delicious meal was created from a simple stone. Have students write a story in which a clever character gathers up the necessary items to make something, such as an ice cream sundae or even a sailboat.

● Monsters love stone slop. Ask children: *What else do you think might be favorite monster dishes?* Then have students create a Monster Menu and describe each dish on the menu in detail.

Aladdin and the Magic Pickle Jar

based on "Aladdin and the Magic Lamp"

CHARACTERS
Narrator • Aladdin • The Pixie of the Pickle Jar • Ed
Airline Pilot • Flight Attendant • Delivery Person

Narrator: After school one day, Aladdin opened up the refrigerator looking for a snack. He found some apples and grapes, but he was not in the mood for fruit. He found chocolate pudding, but he knew he would get in trouble if he ate it without permission. Near the back of the fridge, he spotted a jar marked "Mr. Giggle's Brand Magic Pickles."

Aladdin *(to himself)*: Hmm. How interesting. I don't think I like pickles. But I've never tried a magic pickle. I'm sure this is an acceptable and nutritious snack. I'll be trying something new besides.

Narrator: He opened the jar, fished out a pickle, and took a bite. It was very flavorful, kind of like chocolate mixed with popcorn. Suddenly, a strange elf-like creature appeared. It had blue skin and wings, and it hovered in the air.

Aladdin: Who are you?

The Pixie of the Pickle Jar: I am the Pixie of the Pickle Jar. Every time you eat a magic pickle, you summon me. Your wish is my command.

Aladdin: Hmmm. Let's see. I wish I was the coolest kid in the world.

Pixie: She-leel, she-lyle, she-layle, she-land. I grant Aladdin's wish to be the coolest kid in the world.

Narrator: Poof! Pow! Just like that, Aladdin found himself inside an igloo. Across from him sat a boy wearing a very heavy winter coat.

Aladdin: Where am I? Who are you?

Ed: You're at the North Pole. My name is Ed. It's beautiful outside today, 28 degrees and snowing. Hey, do you want to go sledding? We could make snow angels. Or we could have a snowball fight.

Aladdin: This is not exactly what I meant by "coolest kid in the world." I have to get out of here. I want to go home.

Narrator: Aladdin noticed that he still had his jar of magic pickles. So he took a bite out of another one. The Pixie appeared, shivering.

Pixie: M-m-master, you called? I am the Pixie of the Pickle Jar. Your wish is my command.

Narrator: Sometimes Aladdin had imagined what it would be like to fly. He would just spread out his arms like the wings of a bird. He would pretend he could go up in the air, above his house, above his town.

Aladdin: I wish I could fly to wherever I wanted to go.

Pixie: Abra-kibbiz, abra-kebly. I grant Aladdin's wish to fly.

Narrator: Poof! Pow! Just like that, Aladdin found himself sitting in an airplane.

Pilot: Welcome to Gherkin Express Airlines. We're on a direct flight from the North Pole to your hometown. We'll be reaching an altitude today of nearly 175,000 feet. Our travel time will be approximately three weeks. So sit back and enjoy the trip. In a few minutes, attendants will be making their way through the cabin with in-flight beverage service.

Aladdin (to himself): Three weeks! Who ever heard of a three-week flight! This is terrible. This is not what I meant when I said I wanted to fly.

Flight Attendant (smiling): Can I get anything for you, sir? Can I offer you a glass of fresh pickle juice? Or would you rather have a soft drink? We have Pucker Up Cola, diet and regular.

Aladdin: Could I just have a glass of water, please?

Flight Attendant: Would you like a pickle wedge in that?

Aladdin: No, thanks!

Narrator: Aladdin noticed that he still had his jar of magic pickles. There were two pickles left.

Aladdin (to himself): I've had enough of this silliness. I wish to be cool, I wind up in an igloo. I wish I could fly, I wind up on an airplane. I'm going to make a wish that the Pixie cannot mess up.

Narrator: Aladdin bit one of the magic pickles. Instantly, the Pixie appeared in the empty seat beside him.

Pixie: This is a great movie they are showing, don't you think? Stuart Pickle, one of my favorites.

Aladdin: Yes, it is just great. Now I have a new wish, and I want you to listen very carefully.

Pixie: Your wish is my command.

Aladdin: Okay then. I wish I had my own toy store.

Pixie: Bibble, telfoo, babble, telfor. I grant Aladdin's wish for his own toy store.

Narrator: Poof! Pow! Just like that, Aladdin found himself in the living room of his home. For several minutes, nothing happened. Then the doorbell rang and Aladdin answered it.

Delivery Person: Good afternoon. I'm here from UPS, United Pickle Service. I have a package for a Mr. Aladdin. Could you please sign this form? Now please sign this duplicate form. Now please sign this triplicate form. Okay then. Here is your package, sir. Have a very nice afternoon.

Narrator: Aladdin's box was very small. He tore it open as fast as he could. Inside, he found a tiny model of a grocery store. When he looked carefully, he could see tiny items lined up on the shelves: tiny boxes of cereal, tiny cans of soup, and tiny jars of pickles. Pickles, pickles, pickles!

Aladdin *(to himself):* I ask for my own toy store and what do I get? I get a store that is a toy. I get it! A toy store!

Narrator: Aladdin had one magic pickle left. He took a bite. Immediately, the Pixie appeared. The Pixie was sitting in his living room, in his favorite chair, playing a video game.

Aladdin: I've made three wishes, and not one turned out as I expected. I feel cheated. What do I need to do to get a good wish?

Pixie: You have to word your wish very carefully.

Aladdin: Okay. I think I have a good wish. I think I've figured out a way to get everything I want. Are you listening?

Pixie: I'm listening, sir.

Aladdin: Are you ready?

Pixie: Ready, sir.

Aladdin: I wish for three new pickles in this magic jar.

Pixie: Rickely roo, tickely tickles. I grant Aladdin three new pickles.

Narrator: Poof! Pow! Just like that, there were three new pickles in the jar. Aladdin fished one out and took a bite.

Aladdin *(to himself):* Hmmm. These don't taste like chocolate mixed with popcorn.

Narrator: Aladdin took another bite and another, but the Pixie did not appear. He ate another pickle. Still no Pixie.

Aladdin *(to himself):* Oh, I get it. The Pixie said that I had to make my wish very carefully. I wished for three more pickles in the jar. But I forgot to wish for three more magic pickles.

Narrator: Aladdin was not as unhappy as he'd expected. He was tired of dealing with the Pixie, and he was tired of having his wishes turn out in weird ways. Besides, he found that he kind of liked the taste of pickles. He reached into the jar and pulled out another one.

Aladdin *(to himself):* Mmmm. These pickles are not so bad. In fact, they are kind of tasty.

The End

Aladdin and the Magic Pickle Jar

History of the Tale

The original story—"Aladdin" or "The Wonderful Lamp"—is from *The Arabian Nights* or *A Thousand and One Nights*, a collection of tales with origins in European, Persian, Indian, and Chinese folklore. The premise of the collection is that a woman named Scheherazade is scheduled to be executed by order of the king. To spare her life, she makes up a series of fascinating tales, always leaving off at exactly the right point in order to keep the king in suspense. In this way, she is able to stay alive for 1,001 nights. In the end, the king is so impressed by her storytelling abilities that he spares her life. The original Aladdin features one of the most fanciful notions of all time, a genie that appears when a magic lamp is rubbed. The genie grants Aladdin a series of wishes: a grand feast, piles of gold coins, and the affections of a princess.

Vocabulary Boosters

This story contains several words that may be new to students:

nutritious (*adj.*): description of food that is good for your health

gherkin (*noun*): a pickle, often a very small one

duplicate (*noun*): a second copy of something. "Triplicate" means a third copy.

Discussion Starters

● Encourage students to imagine themselves in Aladdin's place. Ask: *What if you could have three wishes? What would you wish for? People always say they would use their third wish to ask for three more wishes. Is that fair?*

● Aladdin kept making wishes, but things never turned out as he expected. In the end, he was kind of glad that there were no more magic pickles. Invite children to think about the role magic played in the folktale. Then ask: *What would you have done if you were in the Pixie's place? How would you have helped Aladdin be granted his three wishes?*

Writing Prompts

● The famous original story of Aladdin features a genie and a magic lamp. This version features a pixie and a magic pickle jar. Ask each student to make up his or her own character. It could be the crab in the magic cookie jar, for example. Then have children write a story about how the character grants three wishes.

● In this story, Aladdin has to choose his words very carefully. Invite students to think of a wish. Then create a Wish Contract. A wish for a toy store, for example, might include the following in the Wish Contract: "This has to be a large, real store. Real people have to work in it. It has to be full of real toys." Encourage children to write down careful instructions so that they are sure to be granted their wishes.

The June Bug and the Flea

based on "The Grasshopper and the Ant"

CHARACTERS
Narrator • Felix the Fiddlin' Flea • Jack the June Bug
Bugville Residents: Ant Ann, Spider Manny, Mandy the Moth
Sticky Treaters: Millicent the Millipede, Bailey Beetle, Wally the Wasp
Clyde, the Crooning Cockroach • Bea Bee

Narrator: Jack the June Bug and Felix the Fiddlin' Flea could not have been more different. Jack was the manager of a store that sold tiny baby buggies for little baby bugs. He worked all the time. Felix was a fun-loving flea who enjoyed playing his fiddle. He goofed off all the time.

As you might imagine, Bug Day was a huge holiday in Bugville. All the bugs had the day off from work and from school.

Felix the Fiddlin' Flea: I have a great Bug Day planned. I know this dog, a poodle. I plan to burrow into his fur for the day. I'll go wherever the poodle goes. It will be a vacation. Hey, what do you have planned, Jack?

Jack the June Bug: Bug Day is a big waste of time. I'm going to go to the store. I plan to spend the day polishing up the bug baby buggies.

Narrator: On Bug Day, as promised, Jack headed off to work. He held his briefcase with one leg and walked with his other five legs. Everyone else was out having fun.

Ant Ann: Happy Bug Day, Jack! I'm so excited. I'm going to a picnic today with three thousand of my closest relatives. I'll see Ant Stella and Ant Rose and Ant Tina and Ant Agnes . . . .

Jack (interrupting): Have a nice day, Ant Ann. I'm late for work.

Spider Manny: Hi, Jack! I just love Bug Day. I'm going to spend the entire day surfing the Web. What do you have planned, Jack?

Jack: Isn't it obvious? I'm going to work. There are bug baby buggies that need to be polished.

Mandy the Moth: Hi, Jack! There's this pretty red sweater in Mrs. Periwinkle's closet. I've been eyeing it for months. Today, I'm going to eat it! Happy Bug Day, Jack!

Jack: I have work to do. Bug Day! Bah, humbug!

Narrator: Bug-O-Ween was another popular holiday in Bugville. All the bug kids went from house to house, saying "Sticky treat." They collected melted, gooey candy, which was their favorite kind, of course.

Felix: I have a big bag full of melted candies. I kept it out in the sun all day long. I have melted chocolate and melted caramel and melted nougat. Bug-O-Ween is my favorite holiday. I just love handing out candy. I love to see the happy looks on the faces of those cute little bugs.

Jack: Bug-O-Ween is a ridiculous holiday. If young bugs want melted candy, they should work hard and earn money to buy it themselves. When I was a boy I got up every morning at six, I stood up on my own six legs, and I went to work on an ant farm. The job paid one penny an hour. I didn't waste that money on candy either. No, not in my day. I saved those pennies. That can really add up. One hundred pennies equals one dollar.

Felix: One dollar! Big whoop! If I needed a dollar I'd just borrow it . . . from you.

Narrator: On Bug-O-Ween, Jack's doorbell rang. He opened it up and saw three sticky treaters standing there.

The Sticky Treaters *(all together):* Sticky treat! Sticky treat! Sticky treat!

Jack: Go away, bugs. I have nothing here for you.

Millicent the Millipede: Don't you like my costume, sir? I'm a millipede and I'm dressed up as a centipede. Don't you think that's cool?

Jack: It's very inventive. Now, run along.

Bailey Beetle: Hey mister, don't you have anything in your house? Don't you maybe just have a half-empty jar of peanut butter that we could crawl around in?

Jack: I said I have nothing here for you. Now shoo, bugs, shoo!

Wally Wasp *(flexing his stinger):* Well, I oughta . . . I have a half a mind to . . . if this wasn't Bug-O-Ween, I'd . . . I'd . . . I'd show him.

Narrator: During autumn, Bugville's event of the season was the Big Bug Hoedown. It was held in a cornfield right behind Jack the June Bug's house. Felix the Flea played his fiddle. Clyde the Crooning Cockroach sang songs. All the bugs from Bugville danced and carried on. The Big Bug Hoedown always lasted late into the night.

Clyde the Cockroach *(crooning):* Once I loved a little mosquito. She was my red, red rose. She had dainty little feet-o and a stinger on her nose.

Jack *(opening his door):* Quiet down! Stop making so much noise. Some of us have to go to work in the morning.

Narrator: The residents of Bugville ignored Jack. Felix kept playing his fiddle. Clyde just kept crooning. The bugs kept right on dancing the jitterbug under the big autumn moon.

Clyde *(crooning):* Once I loved a little earthworm. She played the tambourine. She could dance the jitterbug and twist like a dancing queen.

Jack *(opening his door)*: Stop that racket! This is my last warning. If I have to come out again, I'm bringing my bug spray.

Bea Bee: C'mon Jack, honey. You've got to learn to enjoy yourself. How about dancing with me. I think you'll find that dancing is fun, honey.

Narrator: Now it so happened that Bea Bee was the most popular bee in the whole hive. She was smart and funny and as pretty as a bee could be. Jack the June Bug could not resist. He agreed to dance with Bea Bee. To his surprise, he really enjoyed himself.

Jack: I can't believe it. Clyde is a great singer. Felix plays the fiddle so well. I just can't help myself. It makes my six legs want to move. I'm one bad boogeying bug. I'm having fun! I'm having fun! By the way, Bea Bee, you look beautiful.

Bea Bee: You're not too bad yourself, honey.

Narrator: The moral of the story: All work and no play makes Jack a dull bug.

The End

The June Bug and the Flea

History of the Tale

The June Bug and the Flea is based on one of Aesop's most popular fables, "The Grasshopper and the Ant." Aesop was a Greek storyteller who lived during the sixth century B.C. His original fable features a hardworking ant that stores up seeds all summer long. Meanwhile, a grasshopper hops about, playing and singing, not worrying about the future. When winter comes, the grasshopper pays the price for being so fancy-free. *The June Bug and the Flea* inverts the moral of Aesop's original fable. It features a bug that works too hard and forgets to stop and have fun. This fractured folktale also mixes in elements of Charles Dickens's *A Christmas Carol*, which introduced the unforgettable character Ebenezer Scrooge. Scrooge disapproved of Christmas, just as Jack the June Bug disapproves of Bugville's various holidays. Fittingly, as a resident of Bugville, Jack echoes Scrooge's famous complaint, "Bah, humbug." In the end, both characters learn to loosen up and enjoy life.

Vocabulary Boosters

This story contains several words that may be new to students:

dainty (*adj.*): something that is both small and lovely

croon (*verb*): to sing, especially in a romantic way

humbug (*noun*): nonsense or foolishness

Discussion Starters

● The original fable "The Grasshopper and the Ant" was about the value of hard work. The fractured folktale *The June Bug and the Flea* is about the need for fun. Ask students if they lean one way or the other on this issue. Is it important to find the right balance?

● Jack the June Bug works at a store that sells baby buggies for bugs. "Bug baby buggies" is certainly a tongue twister! Just try saying it three times fast. Ask children to come up with other tongue twisters.

Writing Prompts

● *The June Bug and the Flea* features a moral: "All work and no play makes Jack a dull bug." Many other stories have morals, such as "the early bird gets the worm." Invite students to think of a moral for a story. It should be something that teaches a useful lesson. Then have children write a story with that moral in mind.

● Bugs make great story characters. They do all kinds of strange and interesting things: flying, hopping, spinning webs. Have students write bug stories. If you like, children can fracture an old fairy tale or a popular book or even a movie by turning the characters into bugs. They could write *Bug-a-Rella*, for example, or *Harry Spider and the Doodlebug's Stone*.

The Prince Frog

based on "The Frog Prince"

CHARACTERS

Narrator • **Lilly Paddington** • **Rachel Twoshoes**
Stu Paddington, Lilly's Brother • **Prince Albert von Hoppinger**

Narrator: Lilly Paddington loved frogs. It was that simple. She had a frog doll, a frog wristwatch, a frog toothbrush, and a frog backpack.

About the only thing Lilly didn't have was a pet frog. It was time for that to change. It was a beautiful spring Saturday. Today, Lilly decided, she was going to catch a frog. She filled an empty jar with leaves and added a little water. She cut holes in the top for air. As Lilly and her dad were heading off to find a frog, she ran into her friend Rachel Twoshoes.

Lilly Paddington: Hi, Rachel.

Rachel Twoshoes: Hi, Lilly. Where are you going with a jar filled with leaves?

Lilly: I'm going to catch a pet frog.

Rachel: Yuck. Why? Frogs are slimy. They totally gross me out.

Lilly: You just don't appreciate them. They have the coolest-looking green skin and cutest-looking little pop-eyes. I love frogs!

Rachel: Personally, I love puppies. Suit yourself. I'll bet the pond in the big field near school is just hopping with frogs.

Lilly: That's a good idea. If I catch two, do you want me to bring you one?

Rachel: No way! Don't even joke about that!

Narrator: Lilly and her dad headed off toward the pond. Along the way, she ran into her older brother, Stu. He was shooting baskets.

Lilly: Hi, Stu.

Stu Paddington: Sis, what are you up to? How come you're walking around with a jar full of leaves?

Lilly: I'm planning to catch a frog. It will make a great pet.

Stu: You don't just catch a frog, Sis. Frogs are hard to spot. They hide in muddy water. If you find one, they quickly hop away. You can try to catch a frog, Sis. But I don't think you'll have much luck.

Lilly: If I find one, I think I'll put it under your pillow.

Stu: That's not cool. Don't even joke about that!

Narrator: They continued on their way to the pond. When they arrived, Lilly tried to find a frog. She couldn't see one anywhere. Maybe her brother was right. Frogs were hard to find.

But Lilly did see the oddest-looking man sitting on a park bench near the pond. He was wearing a long purple robe. On his head, he wore a crown. He looked friendly, but also very strange.

Lilly: Who are you?

Prince Albert von Hoppinger: I'm Prince Albert von Hoppinger, a member of the royal family of the country of New Croakerland. Who are you? Why are you carrying a glass jar full of leaves?

Lilly: I'm Lilly. I'm trying to catch a pet frog.

Prince Albert: A frog? Oh my. Frogs are the most devious creatures. They are always hopping this way and that. No, I think maybe you would be happier with a hamster.

Lilly: I don't want a pet hamster. I have my heart set on a frog.

Narrator: Lilly was getting hungry for a snack. She reached into her green frog backpack. She found an old, mostly empty package of chocolate kisses. There was just one left. She started to unwrap its foil package.

Prince Albert: Hey, a chocolate kiss. Those are my favorite. I'll bet I love chocolate kisses as much as you love frogs. Can I have one?

Lilly: But this is my last one.

Prince Albert: If you'll give me that chocolate kiss, I'll teach you a trick. It is guaranteed to land you a frog.

Lilly (*handing Prince Albert the chocolate kiss*): Okay. This better be a good trick.

Narrator: The prince finished unwrapping the chocolate kiss. Then he popped it in his mouth. In a flash, he was transformed into a frog.

Prince Albert: Ribbit, ribbit, ribbit.

Narrator: Prince Albert, now a frog, sat there puffing out his cheeks. He looked like a very friendly frog. Lilly knew he would make a good pet. She picked him up and plopped him into the jar. Then she ran all the way home. Her brother Stu could not believe Lilly's luck.

Stu: That's amazing! How did you manage to catch one?

Lilly: It was easy. I gave a prince a kiss, and he turned into a frog.

The End

The Prince Frog

History of the Tale

"The Frog Prince" is a traditional European folktale popularized by the Brothers Grimm. It features a princess who is amusing herself by playing with a golden ball in the forest. The golden ball falls into a well. A talking frog promises to retrieve it. In exchange, he demands a kiss. The princess is resistant to the idea but finally agrees. The frog fetches her golden ball from the well. In return for the favor, she kisses him and—in an all-time classic twist—he turns into a prince. The pair fall in love and live happily ever after.

Vocabulary Boosters

This story contains several words that may be new to students:

appreciate (*verb*): to have good feelings about someone or something

devious (*adj.*): sly and tricky

transform (*verb*): to change; to become something else

Discussion Starters

● Lilly loves frogs. Her friend Rachel thinks frogs are gross. Ask students if they have interests that others don't appreciate. Maybe someone enjoys playing the tuba. Perhaps someone else likes to make giant balls out of tinfoil. If it's fun, does it really matter what other people think?

● Ask children what kind of pets they have. *Does anyone have a really unusual pet, such as a tarantula?* As a class, talk about what kinds of pets students would like to have. Where would they keep them? What would be good names? Do some animals make poor pets because they belong in the wild?

Writing Prompts

● Invite children to write an opposite story. For example, the original folktale "The Frog Prince" features a princess who kisses a frog. The frog turns into a prince. *The Prince Frog* is the opposite. A prince turns into a frog. One of the best ways to make up a new story is to turn an old story upside down. Encourage each student to think of his or her favorite story. Maybe a child likes "The Three Little Pigs." The opposite story might feature three little wolves and a big bad pig. Then have students write their own opposite stories.

● Character names are very important. For example, Lilly Paddington is a girl who loves frogs. Her name is similar to *lily pad,* a favorite dwelling place for frogs. The prince is named Albert von Hoppinger. Ask students: *Doesn't "Hoppinger" remind you of a frog?* Invite children to think of three really descriptive character names. Then have students write a story featuring those three characters.

Queen Midas

based on "King Midas"

CHARACTERS

Narrator • Maldor, the Royal Magician • Queen Midas
Millie, the Queen's Faithful Attendant
Rudy, the Royal Photographer • Five Royal Soccer Team Players

Narrator: Queen Midas loved to be entertained. On this particular night, the royal magician was putting on a show. He made an apple disappear into thin air and pulled a rabbit from a hat.

Maldor, the Royal Magician: Queen Midas, it is an honor to perform at your palace. If you will join me on the stage, I have a special trick meant just for you.

Narrator: Queen Midas walked up onto the stage and stood beside Maldor the Magician.

Maldor: My queen, what is your favorite thing in the whole wide world?

Queen Midas: Hmmm. Let's see. Chocolate, I guess. Yes, I am sure of it: chocolate.

Maldor: Good answer. Now, my queen, if you will just drink this potion, you will have the magic touch. Everything that you touch will turn into chocolate.

Narrator: Maldor handed Queen Midas a small bottle of potion marked "Magic Fingers, Chocolate Version." The queen drank it down in one quick gulp.

Queen Midas: That was delicious, kind of like a chocolate milkshake. But I don't feel any different.

Maldor: You may not feel any different. But you are different now, my queen. I'll demonstrate. First, I'll just make that apple reappear. Presto! Here it is. Now, if you'll just touch your finger to it.

Narrator: Queen Midas touched the apple. Instantly, it turned into a chocolate apple. Millie, the queen's faithful attendant, and everyone else in the royal ballroom, gasped in amazement. Queen Midas took a bite out of the chocolate apple. It was delicious.

Queen Midas: This is incredible. Anything I touch turns to chocolate. Millie, bring me that loaf of bread from the table over there.

Millie, the Queen's Faithful Attendant: Yes, Your Highness.

Narrator: Millie brought the loaf of bread. Queen Midas touched it and instantly it turned into chocolate. The queen took a bite; it was good stuff.

Queen Midas: Millie, bring me that fork.

Millie: Yes, Your Highness.

Queen Midas: No, Millie. Not just "Your Highness." From now on, I want you to address me as "Your Chocolate Highness."

Millie: Yes, Your Chocolate Highness.

Narrator: Millie brought over the fork. Queen Midas touched it. It changed in a flash. It still looked exactly like a silver fork, and a very fancy one at that. It had all kinds of curlicues and details. But now the fork was perfectly formed in chocolate. Queen Midas took a bite. Scrumptious!

Queen Midas: Millie, go get a dozen eggs. And some marbles. Oh, and be sure to get some paper clips. Find a feather. You simply must find a feather.

Millie: Yes, Your Chocolate Highness.

Queen Midas: No, Millie. Not just "Your Chocolate Highness." From now on, I want you to address me as "Your Rich Creamy Super-Duper Delightful Chocolate Highness."

Millie: Yes, Your Rich Creamy Super-Duper Delightful Chocolate Highness.

Narrator: Millie brought all the items that Queen Midas had requested. One by one, the queen touched the eggs and the marbles and the paper clips and the feather. They all turned into chocolate. The queen wolfed them down. Soon she had eaten so much that she was growing tired. Millie accompanied the queen upstairs to help her prepare for bed.

Queen Midas: Millie look! I just touched my bedpost. It turned into dark chocolate, just like the dark wood! Mmmmm. Delectable! Look now, Millie! I touched my pillow. It turned into a big fluffy chocolate candy with cream filling. What a delight!

Narrator: Soon the queen fell asleep. When she awoke, her chocolate mattress sagged. The chocolate sheets that covered her chocolate bed had melted. During the night, Fluffy the royal cat snuggled up beside her. Fluffy had turned to chocolate. Everything the queen had touched was chocolate. Everywhere she looked—chocolate. She looked in her chocolate mirror and saw that she was a big chocolaty mess.

Queen: Millie, run me a bath at once.

Millie: Yes, Your Rich Creamy Super-Duper Delightful Chocolate Highness.

Queen Midas: You can go back to simply calling me "Your Highness."

Millie: Yes, Your Highness.

Narrator: As soon as Queen Midas stepped into her bath, the water turned into thick chocolate syrup. Turning everything into chocolate was starting to be less fun. The queen got dressed. But every piece of clothing she touched turned into chocolate. Then she went downstairs, dressed in messy, melting, chocolate robes. Still, there was royal business to be done.

Millie: This morning, Your Highness, you are scheduled to meet with the royal soccer team. They have just won the championship. Rudy, the royal photographer, will take your picture.

Rudy, the Royal Photographer: I have a great picture in mind. You are not a typical queen. You are a wild, fun-loving, chocolate-chomping queen. I think you should give each soccer player a high-five. That will be a cool photograph. I can just picture the headline: "Chocolate-covered queen high-fives soccer stars."

Narrator: The messy chocolate queen high-fived each soccer player. As soon as their hands touched, each player's hand turned to chocolate.

First Soccer Player: My fingers! They're like little candy bars. Now my toes are turning into candy bars! Oh no!

Second Soccer Player: I'm all covered with frosting. I'm turning into a double-chocolate layered upside-down cake! Somebody do something!

Third Soccer Player: I feel like a chocolate donut. I don't mean that I'm hungry for a chocolate donut. What I'm trying to say is, I am a donut. Help! Help!

Fourth Soccer Player: I'm turning into a brownie! Save me! Save me!

Fifth Soccer Player: I scream! You scream! We all scream! I'm chocolate ice cream!

Narrator: This was terrible. First the queen had turned Fluffy the royal cat into chocolate. Now she had turned five royal soccer team players into chocolate. She was a royal mess!

Queen Midas: Listen carefully, Millie. Go and fetch Maldor, the royal magician.

Narrator: Millie ran through the palace and returned a few minutes later with Maldor.

Queen Midas: Maldor, this is terrible. I'm turning everything into chocolate.

Maldor: That is a problem. Fortunately, I have a solution. You just need to drink a little of my special Normal Touch Potion. That will turn everything—and everyone—that is chocolate back to normal.

Queen Midas: Oh, thank goodness. Hand it to me at once, Maldor.

Maldor: No, my queen, not so fast. I am going to set the potion down over here. I have to be careful not to touch you right now. Otherwise, I will turn into chocolate. Then we'll be in real trouble.

Narrator: The queen drank down the potion. It tasted like plain old tap water. Then she walked around her palace. She touched Fluffy, the soccer players, her sheets, her mirror. Everything went back to normal.

Queen Midas: What a relief! I love chocolate more than anything in the world. But that doesn't mean I want the whole world to be chocolate!

The End

Queen Midas

History of the Tale

The original is "King Midas," an ancient Greek myth. The king is granted a wonderful new magic power. Everything he touches turns to gold. At first, this gift gives King Midas great pleasure. He touches a stone and a twig; immediately they turn to gold. But Midas's problems begin when he tries to eat. Every dish he touches turns to gold. Fearing that he will starve, Midas begs the gods to take away his magic power. He is instructed to wash himself off in a river—an act that removes his magic power. According to the myth, King Midas's bath also explains why water has a golden color at certain times of day. In modern times, the story of King Midas remains popular. Someone who has good business instincts is often described as having the "Midas touch." Often forgotten is the fact that the original version was a cautionary tale. It warned about the dangers of too much of a good thing.

Vocabulary Boosters

This story contains several words that may be new to students:

attendant (*noun*): a person whose job is to help another person

wolf (*verb*): to eat quickly and hungrily, like a wolf

delectable (*adj.*): unusually tasty and delicious

Discussion Starters

● Everyone loves chocolate. But Queen Midas had a tough time when absolutely everything she touched turned into chocolate. Ask students if it's possible to get too much of a good thing. See if they can come up with examples, such as eating too much Halloween candy or sleeping too late.

● This folktale ends with Queen Midas saying, "I love chocolate more than anything in the world. But that doesn't mean I want the whole world to be chocolate!" Talk to the class about balance. Is it good that the world isn't made up of all one thing? What if it were all water or all land? What if it were all forest or all cities? Is it better to have a mix?

Writing Prompts

● In the original myth, King Midas had the golden touch. Queen Midas had the chocolate touch. Invite students to think of some kind of magic touch. Maybe everything that a character touches turns into peanut butter. Ask each child to write a story about the character he or she has created.

● Queen Midas asked that she be called by a very silly title: "Your Rich Creamy Super-Duper Delightful Chocolate Highness." As a class, develop silly titles for ten different people. They can be real or imaginary. For example, Batman might be "Honorable Cave-Dwelling Mask-Wearing Cape-Donning Crime Fighter."

Jack and the Giant Sunflower

based on "Jack and the Beanstalk"

CHARACTERS
**Narrator • Bart, Jack's Friend • Jack • Jack's Mom • Jack's Dad
Baby Jill, Jack's Baby Sister • Caterpillar**

Narrator: Jack was tired of the way his parents nagged him. "Do your homework," said his dad. "Clean your room," said his mom. He was tired of his baby sister. All she ever said was made-up words like "goo goo, ga ga." He was tired of his toys. He was tired of school. Jack was very, very tired.

One day, Jack was walking home from school. He ran into his friend Bart. Bart was riding his bike.

Bart: Hey, Jack-e-o!

Narrator: Bart always greeted Jack the same way: "Hey, Jack-e-o." Jack was tired of this greeting.

Bart: How's it going?

Jack *(wearily):* It's going okay.

Bart: Guess what?

Jack *(even more wearily):* What?

Bart: I have some magic seeds. They're in this little box.

Narrator: This news caused Jack to finally perk up.

Jack: Magic seeds? What do they do?

Bart: If you plant one, it will grow into a giant flower. It could be a giant rose or a huge tulip or an enormous dandelion. You want one? Here, I'll give you one.

Narrator: Bart reached into the box and handed Jack a seed. Jack went home and planted it in his backyard garden. Then he went inside for dinner.

Jack's Mom: How was your day today?

Jack *(bored):* Okay.

Jack's Dad: Did you ride your bike?

Jack: What fun are bikes? You just ride around on them and do nothing.

Jack's Dad: I had a red bike when I was a boy with fancy handlebars and a bell. I loved riding that bike!

Baby Jill: Goo gack, ba ba da!

Narrator: As soon as dinner was over, Jack went out to play in the backyard. To his amazement, a giant plant stalk was climbing up out of the garden. It must have stretched 50 feet into the air. He looked up. At the top was a huge yellow flower. The magic seed had grown into a giant sunflower.
    Jack climbed up the stalk. When he got to the top, enormous yellow petals surrounded him.

Jack: I think I'll try to slide down one of these petals. Weeeeeeeeeeeeee!

Narrator: It was like a long wavy slippery yellow waterslide. At the end, he plopped down into the cushiony middle of the sunflower. It was so much fun.
    Jack stood up and brushed himself off. Just then, he saw an extremely large caterpillar.

Caterpillar: Bizz, buzz, bazz, boy! Sunflowers are fun! Each is a wonderful toy!

Jack *(excited):* You're right. Sunflowers are fun! My dad says he really enjoyed riding his bike when he was my age. Bet he didn't have a 50-foot-tall sunflower to slide around on!

Narrator: Jack spent the next two hours sliding on the sunflower petals. Then he climbed down, walked inside the house, and went to bed. The next day was Saturday, and he got up just in time for breakfast.

Jack's Dad: Today, I need you to help me clean out the garage. Then you can play for the rest of the day.

Jack: Aw, Dad! I don't want to clean out the garage.

Jack's Mom: It is good to have chores. When I was a little girl, I had all kinds of chores. I used to help my mother make cookies, and I always enjoyed that very much.

Baby Jill: Da da da, ap ap bap.

Narrator: Jack helped clean out the garage. Then he went back to the garden and climbed up the sunflower stalk. He slid down one of the petals. There, once again, was the caterpillar.

Caterpillar: Bizz, buzz, bazz, boy! Sunflowers are fun! Each is a wonderful toy!

Jack: Yes, you said that yesterday. But you're right. My mom says she liked doing chores. When she was a little girl, I guess she never got to slide around on a humongous sunflower.

Narrator: Jack slid down the sunflower. Sliding down was fun. But somehow it was not quite as fun as the day before. In fact, it was just a little boring. He played for about an hour, then he climbed back down.

  The next morning, Jack woke up and joined his family for breakfast. He planned to play on the giant sunflower some more.

Jack's Dad: Today, you can play in the yard for a little while. But we're also going to go for a long drive in the country. Won't that be fun?

Jack's Mom: I'm packing a picnic lunch. I'm making your favorite sandwich, peanut butter and jelly.

Baby Jill *(very excited):* Ga ga ga ga ga ga!

Narrator: Before the drive and the picnic, Jack went out and climbed the giant sunflower. He slid down one of the petals. Yet again, the caterpillar was there.

Caterpillar: Bizz, buzz, bazz, boy! Sunflowers are fun! Each is a wonderful toy!

Jack: Yes, you've said that several times now. Don't you ever say anything else?

Caterpillar: Bizz, buzz, bazz, boy! Sunflowers are fun! Each is a wonderful toy!

Narrator: Jack played on the sunflower. This time, he was only up there for about five minutes. Then he climbed down. Just when he got to the bottom, the magic sunflower disappeared. Jack found that he did not even care very much.

   He went on the outing with his family and ate a delicious picnic lunch. When Jack arrived back home, Bart was in front of his house, sitting on his bicycle.

Bart: Hey, Jack-e-o!

Narrator: Jack was surprised. He discovered he actually liked having Bart call him "Jack-e-o."

Bart: Hey, I have some magic stones. Do you want to check one out?

Jack: I don't think so. Why don't we just ride our bikes?

The End

Jack and The Giant Sunflower

History of the Tale

● In "Jack and the Beanstalk," Jack trades his mother's cow for some magic beans. He plants them and a tall beanstalk grows. When he climbs to the top, he discovers a castle inhabited by a giant and filled with treasures, such as a talking harp and a hen that lays golden eggs. Jack learns that the castle and all its contents once belonged to his father, a prince, who was killed by the giant.

Repeatedly, Jack climbs the beanstalk and sneaks into the castle, where he hides. Whenever the giant senses that a stranger is around, he says: "Fee Fi Fo Fum. I smell the blood of an Englishman." One by one, Jack manages to take back the various treasures. Finally, Jack goes back for the talking harp. As he is sneaking out of the castle, the harp starts talking and wakes up the giant. The giant pursues Jack down the beanstalk. Jack gets to the bottom first, grabs an axe, and cuts down the beanstalk. The giant falls to his death. Meanwhile, Jack has rescued all the treasures and has returned them to their rightful owner, his mother.

Vocabulary Boosters

This story contains several words that may be new to students:

perk up (*verb*): to get back one's energy or return to being in a good mood

petal (*noun*): one of the little leaves of a flower

outing (*noun*): a brief trip

Discussion Starters

● Discuss the need for variety with the class. Ask: *Is an activity sometimes the most exciting at the beginning? If you repeat an activity over and over, does it become boring?*

● At first, the magic sunflower was exciting. But as time went by, Jack found that the novelty of sliding down giant sunflower petals had worn off. Talk with students about how feelings can change over time. Ask: *Have you ever received a gift that was exciting at first, but then one day didn't seem exciting anymore? Would you enjoy having a giant sunflower in your yard? Would it ever become boring? Why or why not?*

Writing Prompts

● This story features a talking caterpillar. But what if there were rapping bugs? What would a fly named The Fly Girl say? What kind of rapping would we expect to hear from MC Waterbug? Invite students to think of some bugs, give them rapper names, and write down their raps.

● At the end of the story, Bart offers Jack a magic stone. Ask children: *What do you think would grow from a magic stone? How about a magic marble or a magic gumdrop?* Have each student dream up a magic item and write a story describing what would happen if a person planted the item.

Claynocchio

based on "Pinocchio"

CHARACTERS

Narrator • Suzy • Claynocchio • Mr. Paintwell, Suzy's Art Teacher
Ms. Stern, the Principal • Suzy's Classmates

Narrator: The assignment in Mr. Paintwell's art class was to mold a person out of clay. Suzy had just completed hers. She'd made a very real looking boy with a smiling face, arms and legs, ten fingers, tennis shoes, and a baseball cap. Suddenly, the clay boy seemed to wriggle just a little.

Suzy: Did you just move?

Claynocchio: Did I move? I twitched the tiniest bit and now you seem surprised. Why, I can stand and dance and jump and run. Oh, I can move all right. I can do anything you can do, only I can do it better and faster.

Suzy: But who are you? What is your name?

Claynocchio: I'm Claynocchio. My full name is Claynocchio Washington Superman Cleary Hamm. George Washington is a very distant cousin of mine, on my father's side. I'm also related to Superman. Have you read any books by Beverly Cleary? She's my mother. Do you know Mia Hamm, the soccer player? She's my sister. My little sister. I'm much better at soccer than she is. You can just call me Clay.

Narrator: Suzy noticed that as Claynocchio spoke, his ears kept getting larger and larger.

Mr. Paintwell: What is going on, Suzy? There seems to be some commotion at your desk.

Suzy: Nothing, Mr. Paintwell. I'm just talking to Clayno . . . . I mean I'm working on the clay figure.

Narrator: Then Suzy asked Claynocchio another question.

Suzy: Where are you from?

Claynocchio: Candlewaxia, the eighth continent. It is right below Antarctica in the middle of the Specific Ocean. I traveled here by pumpkin coach, just like Cinderella. If I'm not back by midnight, I turn into someone even cooler and funnier and smarter than I already am.

Narrator: As he talked, Claynocchio's ears were growing still larger. Now Mr. Paintwell was walking around the classroom, looking at his students' clay figures.

Mr. Paintwell: Very interesting, Suzy. He is a pretty normal looking boy with a cap, tennis shoes, and a smiling face. But his ears are a bit out of proportion, don't you think?

Narrator: Just then, Claynocchio stuck out his tongue.

Mr. Paintwell *(shocked):* Did your clay figure just stick his tongue out at me?

Claynocchio: Oh, I stuck out my tongue all right. You're lucky I didn't do worse. When I lived in Africa, I was a lion tamer. Sometimes if the lion did not behave, I would have to tug on his mane. I can lift 100 pounds above my head. With one hand. I can run 120 miles an hour, backward, and while blindfolded.

Narrator: Claynocchio's ears were growing huge. Mr. Paintwell's eyes were getting very wide.

Mr. Paintwell: A talking clay figure. And a very untruthful one. Oh my . . . well, I never . . . something must be done at once.

Narrator: Mr. Paintwell hurried off to see the principal, Ms. Stern. When she learned about Claynocchio, Ms. Stern decided to make an announcement over the intercom.

Ms. Stern *(over the intercom):* There is a clay figure on the loose in Mr. Paintwell's room. He is making all kinds of ridiculous claims. He does not appear to be dangerous. Still, please be careful if he walks into your classroom.

Claynocchio: Walk into your classroom? Who is that Ms. Stern kidding? Try flying into your classroom. All I have to do is flap my ears and I can take off. I'm faster than a jet plane. I traveled to the moon once. It took me five minutes. I landed on the moon before any astronauts ever did. I have also been to Neptune. I look great in a spacesuit!

Narrator: By now, all the kids in Mr. Paintwell's class were staring at Claynocchio. He was getting worked up, talking loudly about how well he could fly.

Classmates: Hey, Claynocchio, can you fly into that tree over there and get my kite down? Hey, fly over here and help me with my math homework.

Narrator: Claynocchio started to flap his huge ears. The motion kicked up a breeze in the classroom. Soon he was so worked up that he believed he could actually fly. He ran to the edge of Suzy's desk and leapt into the air. He hit the ground with a plunk and split in two.

Claynocchio: I was flying really well. Someone swatted me out of the air with a ruler. You are all just jealous because I am so smart and funny and strong and fast. And handsome. You all want big beautiful ears like mine! Put me back together at once. Hey, put me back together!

Suzy: I will put you back together. But on one condition. You have to stop all this lying.

Claynocchio: But I'm the best liar in the whole world. In fact, I'm the best in the whole universe.

Suzy: That may be true. But you're going to have to stop, or else I'll leave you in two halves.

Narrator: Claynocchio agreed. Suzy put him back together. Forever after, he stuck around in Mr. Paintwell's classroom and helped kids work in clay. Sometimes, after Claynocchio had been really good and helpful, Ms. Stern let him get on the intercom and say the morning announcements.

The End

Claynocchio

History of the Tale

Claynocchio is based on the classic "Pinocchio" in which a poor cobbler named Geppetto decides to make a puppet out of a block of wood. It is an unusual block of wood and it cries out as he whittles away. He fashions a puppet, which comes to life. Pinocchio is very mischievous. He sticks his tongue out at Geppetto and taunts him.

After coming to life, Pinocchio gets into various scrapes and misadventures. Famously, whenever the puppet lies, his nose grows longer. In certain versions, Pinocchio rescues Geppetto from the belly of a whale. In all tellings, Pinocchio ultimately resolves to behave and stop telling lies.

Vocabulary Boosters

This story contains several words that may be new to students:

mold (*verb*): to make something into a particular shape

commotion (*noun*): loud and disturbing noise or activity

proportion (*noun*): how one part relates to the whole thing

Discussion Starters

● As a class, talk about the disadvantages of lying and the problems a person can get into, such as appearing foolish and losing the trust of others. Ask children: *Is there anything wrong with lying?*

● Claynocchio claimed that his real name was Claynocchio Washington Superman Cleary Hamm. He lists an interesting mix of relatives. Ask students to think up some characters with fascinating real and imaginary relatives, such as Michelangelo Minnie Mouse. What would these people be like; what kinds of talents might they have?

Writing Prompts

● Claynocchio liked to make up stories about himself. Invite students to write their own imaginary life stories (or describe a recent event). Ask them to be creative and stretch the truth until it snaps in half like Claynocchio did when he tried to fly.

● Pinocchio's nose grew when he lied. In this fractured tale, Claynocchio's lies made his ears grow. Encourage each child to create a character and think of something that happens when that character misbehaves. For example, students could invent a girl whose hair turns green when she's mean to her sister or a dog that gets smaller the louder it barks.

Clinky Planky Tenbo

based on "Tikki Tikki Tembo"

CHARACTERS
Narrator • Mrs. Short, the Teacher
Clinky Planky Tenbo De Horpy Da Sorpy Yorble Yibble Blat
Pinky Poindexter, a Soccer Teammate • Manuel, a Soccer Teammate
Mike the Mouth, Radio DJ • Bunny, a Friend

Narrator: Once there was a girl named Clinky Planky Tenbo De Horpy Da Sorpy Yorble Yibble Blat. That was her name, believe it or not. It gave her terrible trouble. On the first day of school, the teacher would have to read this long name. Whenever anyone said anything to her at all, they had to use this ridiculously long name. Every day was a huge challenge.

Mrs. Short: Good morning, students. I hope you had a nice weekend. I also hope you did the assigned reading about the 50 states. In my hand, I'm holding a quiz. I'm going to pass one out to each of you. You will then have exactly five minutes to answer all the questions. Good luck!

Narrator: Mrs. Short passed out the quizzes. But it was trouble from the beginning for Clinky Planky Tenbo De Horpy Da Sorpy Yorble Yibble Blat. At the top of the test, there was a line for students to write their names. But writing her name took her an extremely long time. Besides, the line wasn't long enough for her entire name.

41

Clinky Planky Tenbo De Horpy Da Sorpy Yorble Yibble Blat *(looking at the clock, whispering to herself):* Oh no! This is terrible. The five minutes is almost up. Okay, first question. What is the capital of Kansas? Topeka, yes, Topeka. Second question. What was the first state?

Mrs. Short: Time's up, class. Put down your pencils. I'm going to collect the quizzes.

Narrator: Mrs. Short picked up the quiz belonging to Clinky Planky Tenbo De Horpy Da Sorpy Yorble Yibble Blat. She stared at it for several moments.

Mrs. Short: Excuse me, little girl in the second row with the curly-brown hair. You only answered the first question. What seems to be the problem?

Narrator: Mrs. Short had figured out that whenever possible she'd call her student with the long name "the little girl in the second row with the curly-brown hair." While still pretty long, that description was easier to say than the girl's full name.

Clinky Planky Tenbo: I spent almost the entire five minutes just writing my name.

Mrs. Short: Why don't you come up with a nickname? My name is Dorothy, but all my friends simply call me Dot. Dot Short. Do you see?

Clinky Planky Tenbo: But what could my nickname be? Clinky? Planky? Clink? None of those nicknames sounds any good. I could try my initials, but together they would be C.P.T.D.H.D.S.Y.Y.B. That sounds like a license plate. I could shorten them to C.P. or C.P.T. But those nicknames don't sound good, either.

Narrator: Later that day, at recess, some of the kids decided to play soccer. The team captains were named Binky Burrell and Pinky Poindexter. Clinky Planky Tenbo De Horpy Da Sorpy Yorble Yibble Blat joined the game, too. Sometimes just saying the names Binky, Pinky, and Clinky Planky Tenbo De Horpy Da Sorpy Yorble Yibble Blat made playing soccer confusing.

Pinky: I just stole the ball from Binky. Manuel, run farther up the field. I'll kick the ball to you.

Manuel: Nice kick, Pinky. Now, get ready, it's coming your way, Clinky Planky Tenbo De Horpy Da Sorpy Yorble Yibble Blat.

Narrator: But by the time Manuel finished saying her full name, Binky had stolen the ball away. She kicked the ball all the way back down the field and scored a goal. The other team won.

That night, at home, Clinky Planky Tenbo De Horpy Da Sorpy Yorble Yibble Blat was lying on her bed listening to the radio.

Mike the Mouth *(in DJ voice):* You're listening to Zip 95, home of the most music. We play all good songs all the time, 24 hours a day, 7 days a week, 365 days a year, and 366 days on leap years, which is every four years, by the way. We have less talk, more music.

Now, I've got a pair of free tickets to the Backwards Boyz to give away tonight. I'm going to give them to the 95th caller. So start dialing. And remember, you're listening to Zip 95, the home of more music.

Narrator: Clinky Planky Tenbo De Horpy Da Sorpy Yorble Yibble Blat loved the Backwards Boyz. She picked up the phone and called Zip 95.

Mike the Mouth: We have a winner for those Backwards Boyz tickets. Congratulations, you are tonight's 95th caller. You must be very excited.

Clinky Planky Tenbo *(screaming):* Yes. I love the Backwards Boyz! I can't believe it! This is so great! I just can't believe it!

Mike: And what is your name?

Clinky Planky Tenbo: Clinky Planky Tenbo De Horpy Da Sorpy . . .

Mike *(interrupting her):* I'm sorry, we're running out of time here on Zip 95. We still have a pair of Backwards Boyz tickets to give away. We'll give them to the very next caller, provided the person has a slightly shorter name.

Narrator: Clinky Planky Tenbo De Horpy Da Sorpy Yorble Yibble Blat was very sad. She had done poorly on her quiz. Her ungainly name had caused her team to lose at soccer. Because of her name's length, she also did not win the Backwards Boyz tickets, even though she was the 95th caller.

The next day she was with her friend, Bunny. The two friends were eating chocolate chip cookies.

Bunny: You look sad.

Clinky Planky Tenbo *(taking a bite of the cookie):* Yes, nothing in my life seems to be going right.

Bunny: Well, maybe you ought to think about a nickname.

Clinky Planky Tenbo *(taking another bite):* But what would my nickname be?

Bunny: Don't give up. Let's think about this. You really like cookies, right?

Clinky Planky Tenbo *(mouth full):* Of course!

Bunny: How about Cookie? That's a good nickname for you. It fits very well.

Clinky Planky Tenbo: Yes, Cookie. I like it. Cookie Planky Tenbo De Horpy Da Sorpy . . .

Bunny *(interrupting):* Why don't you try Cookie, just Cookie.

Narrator: And so it was that Clinky Planky Tenbo De Horpy Da Sorpy Yorble Yibble Blat became Cookie. She went to the Backwards Boyz concert despite losing the free ticket. Jason Forestpond, the band's lead singer, even invited her to come up on stage. "What is your name?" he asked. Then he held the microphone out to her and she said, "Cookie." Everybody cheered!

The End

Clinky Planky Tenbo

History of the Tale

This story is based on the classic Chinese folktale "Tikki Tikki Tembo." That story also features a character with an extremely long name, a boy called Tikki Tikki Tembo No Sarimbo Hari Kari Bushkie Perry Pem Do Hai Kai Pom Pom Nikki No Meeno Dom Barako. One day, this unfortunately named boy falls down a well. His brother tells his mother who tells his father who tells the gardener. Each person uses the boy's entire long name. The gardener gets a ladder and climbs down into the well. But by this time, the boy has drowned. The Chinese folktale teaches common sense with a moral the same as this new fractured version: There are benefits to having a short name. Obviously, the original delivers its moral with a far darker twist.

Vocabulary Boosters

This story contains several words that may be new to students:

challenge (*noun*): a task that is tough or difficult

moment (*noun*): a very short period of time

ungainly (*adj.*): awkward, clumsy, and hard to deal with

Discussion Starters

• Ask members of the class if they know of people with nicknames. *Where do those nicknames come from? Is it fun to have a nickname? Are there certain advantages?*

Are there certain disadvantages, too, such as when a nickname is silly or embarrassing?

• Clinky Planky Tenbo could not think of a nickname. She did not like "Clinky" or "Planky" or any of the other obvious choices. But she happened to like cookies, so "Cookie" wound up being a good nickname for her. Point out that sometimes the obvious choices are not the best. If we keep working on a problem, we can sometimes find a solution that was not so obvious.

Writing Prompts

• Clinky Planky Tenbo De Horpy Da Sorpy Yorble Yibble Blat is a very silly name. Ask each student to think of a character with a silly name and write a story about how the name changed the character's life. Maybe it could be a confusing name, such as a boy named "Hello." Whenever people greeted him, they would have to say "Hello, Hello." If he were walking down the hall in school, every time he heard "hello," he would think someone was calling his name.

• The fractured folktale features a radio disk jockey named Mike the Mouth. Ask children: *What if you could be a DJ? What would you have as your on-air name? Would you invite listeners to call in?* Then have each student create a script of dialogue from one of his or her imaginary radio programs.

Three Silly Goats Gruff

based on "Three Billy Goats Gruff"

CHARACTERS
Narrator • Three Goats • Mysterious Creature

Narrator: The three goats were very hungry. They decided to travel to a place that had plenty of tasty tin cans to munch on. On the way, the goats had to cross a narrow bridge, one at a time.

As the first goat crossed, a sound came from under the bridge. It was kind of a buzzing noise. The goat was startled.

First Goat: What was that? Who's there?

Mysterious Creature *(in a small voice)*: It's only me.

First Goat: Speak up. I can barely hear you.

Creature *(in a small voice)*: I'm yelling as loudly as I can.

First Goat: If you are yelling and your voice is so quiet, I guess I must be on a very tall bridge. I have a question for you, mysterious creature. I'm a good-looking goat, with soft fur and pointy ears. What do you look like?

Creature: Well, I have six legs and a pair of antennae. I have a shell kind of like a turtle's, but mine is bright red with black spots . . . .

First Goat *(interrupting):* Oh no! This is terrifying. Something dangerous is hiding under the bridge . . . a vicious six-legged, red-shelled turtle thing, and it is coming to get me!

Narrator: The first goat ran across the bridge at top speed. Now it was the second goat's turn to cross.

Second Goat: I know you're down there. I know you're hiding beneath the bridge waiting to jump out. Just leave me alone.

Creature: Don't worry, I'm just a . . .

Second Goat *(interrupting):* Don't come any closer. I have a question for you, mysterious creature. I'm a fast-running goat. I can run like the wind. How fast can you run?

Creature: Well, I have six legs, but I don't do much running. Mostly I fly.

Second Goat: Oh me, oh my! A horrifying beast is under the bridge. It is a dangerous, flying, dragon-turtle thing. It probably breathes fire and is coming to get me.

Narrator: The second goat ran across the bridge at top speed. Now it was the third goat's turn to cross.

Third Goat: You don't scare me, dragon-turtle with the weird antennae. I'm a tough old goat. I win every fight. I have just one question for you. Are you ready to rumble?

Creature: I really don't want . . .

Third Goat *(interrupting):* Come out, come out! Put up your six dukes!

Creature: Okay, but I think you're going to surprised.

Narrator: The creature flew out from under the bridge. Sure enough, the goat was very surprised.

Third Goat: But . . . but . . . you're just a little ladybug!

Creature: That is what I was trying to tell you.

Third Goat: But you said you were gigantic. You said you had a hard shell and a long snake-like neck. You said you could breathe fire and shoot poison darts out of your fingertips.

Creature: No, I did not say much of anything. You goats talk a lot, but you are not so good at listening.

Third Goat: I'm sorry. I didn't catch that. Did you say that my fur is glistening? Why, thank you. Thank you very much! Hey, ladybug, would you like to join us and eat some tin cans?

Creature: No, thanks, not today.

Narrator: The third goat continued crossing the bridge and joined the other two.

Creature *(under its breath):* Now those were sure some silly billy goats.

The End

Three Silly Goats Gruff

History of the Tale

The original "Three Billy Goats Gruff" is a classic folktale that has been passed on from generation to generation via the oral tradition. In most tellings, three goats that are brothers cross a bridge to graze in a meadow. Underneath the bridge lives a troll.

The first goat is the smallest. As he crosses the bridge, the troll threatens to eat him. But he begs for his life, pleading that his brother is larger and will make a better meal. The troll lets the first goat go and waits for the second one. But this goat also fends off the troll by explaining that his brother is larger and tastier still. As the third goat crosses, the troll comes out from under the bridge. Indeed, the third goat is largest of the brothers. But he is also tougher and he knocks the troll off the bridge. The troll is never heard from again.

Vocabulary Boosters

This story contains several words that may be new to students:

antennae (*noun, plural*): A pair of feelers that help an insect sense its surroundings

vicious (*adj.*): very mean or cruel

gigantic (*adj.*): large, like a giant

Discussion Starters

● The three goats talked too much and asked too few questions. As a result, they were confused and thought a harmless little ladybug was a poisonous, fire-breathing turtle dragon. Encourage students to think about what happens when people don't ask enough questions. Ask: *Do they wind up with poor information? Do they make poor decisions? Is it dangerous to ask too few questions?*

● The ladybug described itself as having six legs, antennae, big black spots, and wings. Have children take turns describing different animals without naming them. Ask students to give clues, such as sharp teeth or wings. Let classmates guess. The class can also play this game by describing objects, such as television sets or buses.

Writing Prompts

● Even though the ladybug is yelling, it has a very quiet voice. But the first goat says, "If you are yelling and your voice is so quiet, I guess this must be a very tall bridge." This is quite a misunderstanding. Invite students to write a story with a big misunderstanding at the center. For example, one boy tells another: "I'm having a birthday party tomorrow afternoon." But the other boy thinks he said, "I'm having a birthday party tomorrow on the moon." What happens then? Have each child write a story about it.

● Three animals crossing a bridge makes for a good story. Ask students to write a story about three hippos crossing a bridge with a monkey underneath. Encourage students to have fun and make sure their stories have a surprising twist.

The Elves and Young Stu Baker

based on "The Elves and the Shoemaker"

CHARACTERS

Narrator • Stu's Dad • Stu Baker • Stu's Mom • Three Elves

Narrator: The clock in Stu's bedroom was 18 minutes fast. He knew this, but he did not feel like resetting it. Then there was toothpaste. Whenever Stu halfway finished a tube, he simply threw it away and asked his parents to buy a new one. Rolling up toothpaste tubes took effort. It required work. Stu was a very lazy boy.

Stu's Dad: Stu, I would like you to mow the lawn. You promised to do that today. You are supposed to do it once a week. Stu, I don't believe that you have done the chore in months.

Narrator: The lawn was overgrown. The grass was nearly knee-high.

Stu Baker: What a mess. I can't mow this lawn. It will take all afternoon and I won't have any time to play or have fun. I wish the lawn would just mow itself. In fact, I think I'll go play at Jeff's house for one hour. Who knows? When I come back maybe the lawn will be mowed.

Narrator: Stu went to play at Jeff's house. Meanwhile, three small elves appeared out of nowhere. They were all dressed in green. They turned on the lawnmower and set to work.

Three Elves *(singing while they mow):* Ho, ho, ho, hey, hey, hey!
We will mow Stu's lawn today.
Shoo-be-doo, shack-a-lack!
One day soon he'll pay us back.

Narrator: After one hour, when Stu came back, he was amazed.

Stu: I can't believe it! Someone really mowed the lawn while I was gone. I wonder who it could be?

Stu's Dad: Good job, son. I'm very proud of you. Come inside and have a nice cold glass of lemonade.

Narrator: The next day, Stu's mother asked him to clean up after the cat.

Stu's Mom: When we got Mittens, you promised you would help care for her. I always end up having to empty her litterbox. We had an agreement, Stu. I want you to go down to the basement and clean up Mittens's area right now.

Narrator: Stu did not like work of any kind. Cleaning up after Mittens was one of his least favorite tasks.

Stu: Yuck. I don't want to clean up after Mittens. It will take all evening and I won't have any time to play or have fun. I wish this litterbox would just clean itself. In fact, I think I'll go to the other side of the basement for one hour. I'll play video games. When I come back, maybe the litter box will have cleaned itself. Who knows? It happened last time.

Narrator: Stu went off and played video games. Once again, the three elves appeared and cleaned up after Mittens.

Three Elves *(singing while they clean)*: Click, clack, clank, rat-a-tat!
We'll clean up after Stu's cat.
Shish, bang, boom, boog-a-loo!
For us, he'll do a favor, too.

Narrator: After one hour, when Stu returned, he was even more stunned
than before.

Stu: Oh, my! It happened again. Someone cleaned up after Mittens while I
was playing video games. This is great. This means I can have fun all the time
and someone else can do all the work. I wonder who is doing this?

Stu's Mom: I am so proud of you, Stu. Come upstairs, I baked some fresh
brownies and I'll give you one.

Narrator: Two days later, Stu's parents asked him to clean his room.

Stu's Dad: Son, we agreed that you would clean your room once a week.

Stu's Mom: It has been more like a month.

Stu's Dad: Or a year.

Stu's Mom: It is a terrible mess.

Stu's Dad: Stu, you have to clean it at once. No more fun and games
until you complete this chore.

Narrator: Stu did not like any tasks. Cleaning his room was his least favorite of all.
His bed had remained unmade for more than a week. Clothes and toys
were strewn everywhere.

Stu: What a disaster! I can't clean up this room. It will take hours or days even.
I wish this room would just clean itself. I have gotten lucky twice before,
right? Maybe it will happen again.

Narrator: Instead of cleaning his room, Stu decided to hide in the closet.
He waited for whoever cleaned up the last time to show up once again.
Presently, the three elves appeared. Stu could not believe his eyes!

First Elf: What a mess! This is the worst job Stu has given us yet.

Second Elf: I don't think we can do this chore. It is too much work.

Third Elf: You're right. Let's just go home.

Narrator: Stu stepped out from the closet where he had been hiding. He begged the elves to stay.

Stu: Please, please, clean up my room. You did such a good job with the lawn and the litterbox. My parents were so proud of me.

First Elf: Okay, we'll clean your room.

Second Elf: But you are going to have to do us a favor in return.

Third Elf: We'll help you now. But you are going to have to help us later.

Narrator: The elves made Stu's bed, put away his toys, and picked up his socks.

Elves *(singing):* Yeah, yeah, yeah. Right, right, right!
We're cleaning up Stu's room tonight.
Biddly-biddly-boo, badly-badly-bo!
Stu's turn to clean is tomorrow.

Narrator: When the elves finished, they explained the deal to Stu. The next day, he would need to come to their house. They gave him their address at 123 Candy Cane Lane. Stu would have to mow their lawn and clean up the house.

Stu *(muttering to himself):* I got the better part of this deal. I'm very messy and very lazy. They are hardworking elves. I'll bet their house is already very neat. I won't have to do much at all. Besides, they're tiny. I wouldn't be surprised if their lawn is the size of a postage stamp. Mowing it will be a cinch.

Narrator: The next day, Stu rode his bike to 123 Candy Cane Lane. He was shocked. The elves' yard was huge and overgrown with weeds and dandelions. Inside, the house was in shambles. There were pots and pans everywhere, crusted with dried elf food. What a disaster! Stu couldn't believe it. He knew mowing and cleaning were going to take many hours of hard, hard work.

Stu *(singing as he worked)*: Boodly, boodly, boo. Biddly, biddly, bit!
This house looks like a tornado hit.
Eeny, meenie, mine. Oony, noony, yours!
Next time I'll do my own chores.

Narrator: Forever after, Stu did do his own chores. He found that he preferred to clean up his own mess. The elves continued to clean other people's homes. In exchange, those people agreed to clean the house at 123 Candy Cane Lane. People were always shocked to learn that three tiny elves could be so messy.

The End

The Elves and Young Stu Baker

History of the Tale

This tale is based on the "Elves and the Shoemaker," a classic folktale that was popularized by the Brothers Grimm. Most versions feature a poor shoemaker who has only one piece of leather left. He leaves it on his workbench, planning to craft it into a shoe the following day. When the shoemaker awakes, he finds that someone has done the work for him during the night.

He sells the shoe and earns enough money to buy two more pieces of leather. The shoemaker also leaves these pieces out. When he awakes, he finds that they have been crafted into shoes. On the third night, the shoemaker and his wife stay awake and hide behind a curtain to see who is making the shoes. To their surprise, they spy a group of tiny elves wearing tattered clothes. So the shoemaker's wife stitches tiny clothes for the elves. The next night, the couple sets the clothes on the workbench.

The elves had helped the shoemaker during a difficult time. The shoemaker and his wife returned the favor by stitching new clothes for them.

Vocabulary Boosters

This story contains several words that may be new to students:

strewn (*adj*): Spread around in a messy fashion

cinch (*noun, slang*): Something very easy

shambles (*noun*): complete disorder

Discussion Starters

● Young Stu Baker hoped that he could get something for nothing. He thought he could play video games and goof around while the elves did all the work. In the end, he had to do even more work. Cleaning up the elves' house was a real chore. Start a discussion with students about whether it is possible to get something for nothing.

● Is it work not to do work? This is an interesting question. In the fractured folktale, Stu devoted considerable effort to shirking his responsibilities. Ask children: *Is it harder to avoid tasks than to do them? If you put things off, do you wind up having to do more work later?*

Writing Prompts

● Here are some titles: "The Elves and the Dressmaker"; "The Elves and the Salt Shaker"; "The Elves and the L.A. Laker"; "The Elves and the Pie Baker." Have students select one of these titles and write their own fractured folktales.

● In this story, the elves always sang songs while they worked. Ask: *What are some work songs you might sing while doing your homework, cleaning your room, or giving your dog a bath?* Invite each child to think of at least three tasks and write work songs to go with those tasks.

Thaddeus Thumb

based on "Tom Thumb"

CHARACTERS

Narrator • Old Buck, the Cowboy • Thaddeus Thumb
Freddy Fingers, Thaddeus's Friend
Bankrobber • Mrs. Templeton, Thaddeus's Teacher

Narrator: Everyone has heard of Tom Thumb. But people may not know his distant relative named Thaddeus Thumb. Thaddeus Thumb is Tom Thumb's brother's son's sister's daughter's third and youngest child.

Thaddeus Thumb lives in modern times and his adventures are every bit as exciting as those of Tom Thumb. During summer vacations, Thaddeus always goes to camp. Camp has all kinds of fun activities.

Old Buck: Okay, everyone, climb up onto those saddles. Put your feet in the stirrups. Today, we're going to ride the range.

Narrator: All the kids climbed onto their horses. That is, everyone except Thaddeus Thumb. Instead, he mounted his trusty mouse. He used a tiny toy saddle from a cowboy action figure.

Thaddeus Thumb (to his mouse, Whiskers): Whoa, boy! Easy. Good mouse. Good mousey. Okay, giddy-up. Hi ho, Whiskers, away!

Narrator: Suddenly, there was a loud rumbling noise in the distance.

Old Buck: Stampede! I would recognize that sound anywhere. Some of the other horses must have gotten loose from the pen. I want all of you kids to stay here. I'll go round up those runaway horses.

Narrator: Old Buck galloped off as fast as he could. Thaddeus Thumb could not resist a good adventure. He sped off close behind on Whiskers the mouse.

Old Buck: Do my eyes deceive me? Those aren't horses! It's an elephant stampede!

Narrator: About ten elephants were stampeding through the valley. Old Buck turned around in fright. He rode off as fast as his horse would carry him. But Thaddeus Thumb kept on riding, straight toward the runaway elephants.

Thaddeus: Yee haw! Look down, elephants! It's Thaddeus Thumb to the rescue. I'm riding mouseback. I'm going to round you up and drive you home.

Narrator: When the elephants saw the mouse, they stopped in their tracks. Then they turned in terror and ran the other way. Thaddeus Thumb chased them all the way back into town. It turned out they had escaped from the circus. Then he rode his mouse back to camp.

Old Buck: Thaddeus Thumb, you may be the smallest cowboy I've ever seen. I reckon you are also the bravest. As a reward, I've made you a little lasso out of a shoelace.

Narrator: Later in the summer, Thaddeus Thumb's friend Freddy Fingers built a treehouse.

Freddy Fingers: Hey, Thaddeus. Climb up here. It is really cool. There's a great view. You can see the entire neighborhood.

Thaddeus Thumb: I would like to climb up there, Freddy. But I can't. Your treehouse is too high up. I think I'll build a dandelion house instead.

Narrator: Thaddeus Thumb gathered up some toothpicks. Then he climbed up the dandelion stem and built a tiny house.

Suddenly, a breeze kicked up. Thaddeus Thumb grabbed onto one of the little dandelion parachutes and was carried into the air. He rose high above his neighborhood, then high above the town.

Thaddeus Thumb: Wow! Look at that. There's Freddy's house. There's my house. Over there, I see the ball field. People are playing baseball. From up here, they look as tiny as me.

Narrator: The breeze died down and Thaddeus's dandelion parachute began to fall back to the ground. Suddenly, below him he saw a robber running out of the bank. The robber had a bag of money in each hand.

Thaddeus Thumb let go of the dandelion parachute. He dropped onto the robber's shoulder, right next to his ear. Thaddeus Thumb knew he had to think quickly.

Thaddeus: Police! Drop the money right now. Put your hands up.

Narrator: The robber turned around and looked over his shoulder.

Bank Robber: You'll never catch me. I have such a great head start that I can't even see you back there.

Thaddeus: Drop the money at once. Put your hands in the air.

Bank Robber: Where are you? I can hear you. But I can't even see you.

Thaddeus Thumb: Don't you read the newspaper? Everyone on the police force was issued a brand new invisible uniform. I'm wearing my uniform right now. I'm right behind you, but you can't see me. Now, drop the money. Put your hands in the air. You are under arrest.

Narrator: The bank robber was so frightened that he did as Thaddeus Thumb said. Soon afterward, the real police arrived and arrested the robber. Thaddeus Thumb was a hero. The police officers were so grateful that they sewed a tiny uniform for him out of blue felt. Soon, summer ended and Thaddeus returned to school.

Mrs. Templeton: It is the first day of school. Welcome back, students. I hope everyone had a very enjoyable summer vacation.

Narrator: Thaddeus Thumb was starting the third grade. He was the smallest kid in his class. He sat on a huge stack of books so that he could reach his desk. When he wrote, he had to stand on top of the piece of paper. It seemed huge to him. He would push his pencil around. The pencil also seemed huge.

Mrs. Templeton: I would like everyone to write an essay about what they did this summer. I'm sure all of you had various adventures, large and small. Take half an hour and write down some of them.

Narrator: Thaddeus Thumb thought about his adventures. He had been the smallest cowboy his friend Old Buck had ever seen. Who would ever guess that Thaddeus had rode a dandelion parachute high above Freddy Fingers' house? Or, that Thaddeus had stopped bank robbers? The more Thaddeus thought about his summer, the more excited he became about writing and sharing all that he had done.

Thaddeus Thumb *(writing):* What I Did This Summer, by Thaddeus Thumb.

The End

Thaddeus Thumb

History of the Tale

The original Tom Thumb, a German folktale, begins with a married couple who long for a child. The wife says she and her husband would be grateful even if the child were "as small as a thumb." This wish is granted. Tom Thumb winds up getting involved in all kinds of adventures. For example, he falls asleep in a haystack. When he awakes he is in the mouth of a cow that is chewing hay. Tom has to jump about, dodging the cow's teeth. He has to figure out a way to escape. In both the original and fractured tales, the tiny main character uses his size to his advantage and always finds ways to triumph.

Vocabulary Boosters

This story contains several words that may be new to students:

deceive (*verb*): to lie to or mislead someone

issue (*verb*): to give or provide

grateful (*adj.*): full of thanks or appreciation

Discussion Starters

● Old Buck the cowboy planned to round up the stampeding horses. When he learned that elephants, not horses, were stampeding, he was scared. But Thaddeus Thumb was able to round them up while riding on a tiny mouse. Ask: *Do things sometimes work out the opposite of how we would expect?*

● Someone as tiny as Thaddeus Thumb could ride on a mouse. He was able to fly through the air on a dandelion parachute. Ask students to suggest other things a really tiny person could do. What about a giant? For example, a giant might be able to use a tree trunk for a toothpick.

Writing Prompts

● This story includes two of Thaddeus Thumb's adventures. But he had many adventures. Invite children to think of another one and write a sequel, *Thaddeus Thumb II: Return of the Small Wonder*. In this new story, have students make sure that Thaddeus's small size once again helps him to triumph.

● Thaddeus Thumb is a distant relative of Tom Thumb. What about the relatives of other well-known characters? If Superman had a sister, what would she be like? What about the son of Little Red Riding Hood? Maybe he would wear a blue baseball cap everywhere and would get into a scrape with a mean old bulldog. Ask each child to imagine an interesting relative and tell this character's story.

The Pig Who Cried Wolf

based on "The Boy Who Cried Wolf"

CHARACTERS
Narrator • Percy Little • Paul Little • Parker Little • Big Bad Wolf

Narrator: Once upon a time, there were three brother pigs, with the last name Little. The first one was named Percy Little. He lived in a house made out of twigs, foil gum wrappers, and Popsicle sticks. He was a very silly pig and was always playing foolish pranks.

   Paul, the second pig, lived in a plain cottage. He was more sensible than Percy. The third brother, Parker, lived in a brick house. He was the most sensible of the three Little pigs.

   One day, Percy decided to play another of his pranks. He called Paul on his cell phone.

Percy Little: Oh my! Oh no! Help, Paul! Help!

Paul Little: What is it?

Percy: There's a Big Bad Wolf. He's right outside my door. He's threatening to huff. He says he's going to puff. I think he might blow my house down.

Paul: Don't worry, Percy. I'll take care of the wolf. I'll be right over.

Narrator: Paul raced over to Percy's house. When he arrived there was no wolf. Percy fell on the ground and rolled around giggling.

Percy: You fell for it. I got you! You should see the look on your face.

Paul: That's not funny, Percy. You shouldn't call someone up on your cell phone pretending a wolf is out to get you.

Narrator: But Percy didn't listen. The next day he decided to play the same prank on Parker. Percy started up his computer and sent Parker an e-mail.

Percy *(speaking as he writes his e-mail message):* Help, help! A Big Bad Wolf has broken into my home. He stole my cell phone. I'm hiding here in the bedroom sending e-mails. You have to rescue me.

Parker Little *(writing back):* Oh no. This is terrible! Don't worry. I'll be right over.

Percy: Hurry! He's threatening to huff. He says he's going to puff. I think he might blow my house down.

Narrator: Parker raced over to Percy's house. When he arrived, once again, there was no wolf. Once again, Percy fell on the ground and rolled around giggling.

Percy: It works every time. You look even funnier than Paul. A Big Bad Wolf, yeah right. Like one is really going to just show up and start huffing and puffing.

Parker: Laugh now, Percy. This is no way to behave. A wolf may not be blowing your house down. But you're certainly blowing your credibility.

Percy: Credibility. Ooooh, a big word from Parker Little. I think I'll start calling you Professor Parker.

Narrator: Parker stormed out of Percy's house and went home. But Percy seemed to hardly notice. Then, around midnight, he heard a knock at his door.

Percy: Who is it?

Big Bad Wolf: It's the Big Bad Wolf.

Percy: Yeah, right. I recognize your voice, Parker. Nice try. I'm the prankmaster and nobody outpranks me.

Big Bad Wolf *(knocking harder):* Let me in! Let me in!

Narrator: Percy looked through the peephole in his door. It certainly wasn't Paul. It didn't look like Parker. It really was a Big Bad Wolf.

Percy: What do you want?

Big Bad Wolf: I'm here to huff. I'll also be doing some puffing. In the end, I suspect that I will have succeeded in blowing your house down. That's my plan. I'm not going to eat you or anything. But when I'm finished, you will need to find a new abode.

Percy *(shouting):* Help, somebody, help! There's a Big Bad Wolf at my house. He's threatening to blow my house down. Oh, please, somebody help.

Narrator: Percy cried for help. He yelled so loudly that Paul and Parker could hear. But they assumed it was just another of Percy's pranks. He kept on shouting, but nobody came. True to his word, the Big Bad Wolf blew Percy's house down.
    The next morning, Paul and Parker came by to visit. They found Percy sitting sadly in the ruins of his house. They helped him build a new house. But they also gave Percy some advice.

Paul: Never cry wolf as a joke. Pretty soon no one will believe you anymore. Then when a Big Bad Wolf really shows up on your doorstep, no one will help you.

Parker: It is a matter of trust, Percy. We have to be able to believe the things you say. As Paul says, never cry wolf.

Percy: I've learned a very important lesson today. I don't know how to thank you. Paul, Parker, can I offer you each a stick of gum?

Paul: I don't want a stick of your trick pepper gum.

Parker: I'm not falling for that again.

Percy: Okay, okay, sorry, no more pranks. I really have learned my lesson.

The End

The Pig Who Cried Wolf

History of the Tale

This fractured folktale combines the plots of two classics, "The Three Little Pigs" and "The Boy Who Cried Wolf." The first of these is a traditional folktale, passed from generation to generation by storytellers. A variety of written versions now exist, but they all share a similar storyline. Three pigs build three houses—of straw, wood, and brick. The Big Bad Wolf blows down the first two but can't blow down the brick one. The three pigs huddle safely inside. "The Boy Who Cried Wolf" is one of Aesop's fables. In the original, a shepherd boy cries out "wolf" for sport. He enjoys watching the villagers scramble to his aid. But then a wolf really does attack his sheep, and he cries out in vain. The moral of this fractured folktale is the same as Aesop's original: Never cry wolf.

Vocabulary Boosters

This story contains several words that may be new to students:

storm (*verb*): to move in an angry way

credibility (*noun*): a quality that helps people believe in and trust someone

abode (*noun*): a person's home

Discussion Starters

● Parker is angry at Percy for crying wolf when there is no wolf. He tells him it's a "matter of trust." Talk to the class about trust. Ask: *What happens if you repeatedly lie to people or play pranks, as Percy did? After a while, people stop believing you, right? What kinds of problems can happen then?*

● "Never cry wolf" is a great saying. The Greek storyteller Aesop made it up thousands of years ago and people still use it today. Ask students to suggest some other good sayings, such as "the early bird gets the worm." Discuss the various sayings. Where do they come from? What do they mean and are they really true?

Writing Prompts

● "The Pig Who Cried Wolf" is a mixed-up folktale. It throws together parts of two other tales, "The Three Little Pigs" and "The Boy Who Cried Wolf." Mixing up existing stories is a good way to tell a new story. Ask children: *What would happen, for example, if we combined "Goldilocks" and "Snow White"?* Then have students write their own mixed-up folktales.

● What else could someone cry besides "wolf"? What might get you in trouble? You could cry "lion" or "shark" or "tornado." Invite each child to write a story about a boy or girl who cries something besides "wolf." Make sure that the character learns a valuable lesson in the end.